Unusual Prophecies Being Fulfilled

Unusual Prophecies Being Fulfilled

Repeating *the* SIGNS *of the* Days *of* Noah *and* Lot

Tsunamis, Hurricanes, *and* Volcanoes *in* Prophecy

Perry Stone

All Scripture is taken from the New King James Version of the Bible, unless otherwise indicated.

ISBN: 0-9708611-4-1
LOC: 2005922752

Voice of Evangelism Outreach Ministries
P.O. Box 3595
Cleveland, Tennessee, 37320
(423) 478-3456
Fax: 423-478-1392
www.Perrystone.org

Printed in the United States of America
Pathway Press, 1030 Montgomery Avenue,
Cleveland, Tennessee 37311

Contents

Introduction / 9

The Sea and the Waves Roaring / 11

The Shaking of the Nations / 29

Parallels to the Days of Noah / 55

Blood, Fire and Pillars of Smoke / 71

Selective Judgment / 79

Conclusion / 85

Appendix 1: The Protection of the Righteous / 87

Appendix 2: Warnings from the Animals / 90

Appendix 3: America's Tsunami Threats / 93

God is our refuge and strength, a very present help in trouble.

Therefore will not we fear, though the earth be removed, and though the mountains be carried into the midst of the sea;

Though the waters thereof roar and be troubled, though the mountains shake with the swelling thereof. Selah.

There is a river, the streams whereof shall make glad the city of God, the holy place of the tabernacles of the most High (Psalm 46:1-4)

Introduction

I was awakened at 2:30 a.m. on a Friday morning, and was unable to go back to sleep. I sensed the Lord would have me to go to my study, take my Bible and begin reading in the Book of Jeremiah. There had been a major disaster in the Asian region and there were numerous spiritual, theological and prophetic questions pouring into my office by mail and e-mail, asking if this event was mentioned in prophecy and what the prophetic implications are for the future.

For several hours I read the Word and began seeing the amazing correlation between the backslidings of ancient Israel and the sins of many nations in the Pacific Rim. I began to see how the patterns of God's judgment on ancient Israel seemed to be repeating themselves in our generation. My research began to answer my own questions. Suddenly, the picture became quite clear, as I matched God's warnings through the Hebrew Prophets with New Testament prophecies that predicted trouble on the sea and disaster from destructive winds, occurring in the season prior to the return of Christ.

At 4:00 a.m., the Holy Spirit impressed me to write down what He was giving me. I also felt the need to get this teaching into the hands of as many people as possible. One of the best ways to do this is through the printed page.

This is the first in a series of books which will be printed dealing with *Unusual Prophecies Being Fulfilled.* In each volume I will take several unusual prophecies which deal with the same theme, and develop a prophetic picture of how these passages are beginning to come to pass in our generation. This will, hopefully, give the reader a better understanding of the prophetic times and seasons.

The fact that this generation is now able to perceive and understand the many ancient prophecies of the Bible, is a fulfillment of Daniel's prediction in Daniel 12:4:

> But you, Daniel, shut up the words, and seal the book until the time of the end; many shall run to and fro, and knowledge shall increase (Daniel 12:4).

As we continue to walk the path that concludes with the glorious return of Jesus Christ, it is important for us to have the same spirit the sons of Issachar had when it was said they "had understanding of the times, to know what Israel ought to do" (1 Chronicles 12:32). I believe our ministry has a mandate from the Holy Spirit to help present an understanding of the prophetic times and seasons in which we are living. The world has, and will have, many questions. We, the believers, need to have the answers.

A Servant of the Lord

Perry Stone, Jr.

There will be signs in the sun, in the moon, and in the stars . . . on the earth distress of nations, with perplexity, the sea and the waves roaring. . . Then they will see the Son of Man coming in a cloud with power and great glory (Luke 21:25-27).

1

The Sea and the Waves Roaring

On Sunday, December 26, 2004, at 7 a. m., something unplanned and unexpected occurred deep beneath the Indian Ocean. Off the coast of Sumatra, Indonesia, the entire Aceh province was jarred by a 9.0-magnitude earthquake. When the shaking ended, the people on land knew they had experienced an earthquake. Within minutes, the water had risen several inches, washing numerous fish up on the shore. This unusual incident attracted many who ran to the shoreline to catch the fish.

In hundreds of South Asian vacation resorts, children had been splashing in the waves while dads rubbed sunscreen on moms. Others lazily basked in the warm sun, enjoying a perfect day at the beach. Thousands of individual tourists and their families, representing many nations, were enjoying a Christmas vacation in various countries around the Indian Ocean rim.

Suddenly, a violent wave inundated the entire coastline. Before mothers could grab their children and before sunbathers could escape with their belongings, the tide rose and thousands were caught in the muddy, swirling waves like a helpless insect, struggling in a spider's web. Without warning, the 30- to 35-foot wave, a tsunami, appeared, tossing people and objects on the beaches in its devastating fury. This 2004 Indian Ocean tsunami is estimated to have released the energy of 23,000 Hiroshima-type atomic bombs.

This tragedy was catastrophic. More than 200,000 people lost their lives in Indonesia, Sri Lanka, India, Thailand, Somalia, Myanmar, Malaysia, Maldives, Seychelles, Tanzania, Bangladesh—even South Africa and Kenya, 3,200 miles away. Because of limited communication technology in the area and no large warning systems, the surrounding nations with large coastal areas experienced the worst natural disaster in their history.

Within 24 hours, the Western world added *tsunami* (pronounced soo-nom-ee) to its vocabulary. A Japanese word that comes from *tsu* meaning "harbor" and *nami,* meaning "wave," the word means "the waves which come into the harbor."

Within moments of the Indian Ocean disaster, news networks and news reporters were calling scientists, seismologists and geologists to request interviews, information and background briefings on the subject. Within hours the entire world began to hear about tsunamis and tectonic plates.

THE TECTONIC PLATES

If a person takes a large paper map of the world and cuts out the continents, they can be connected together like pieces of a jigsaw puzzle. Many people, including scientists, believe the continents were once united as one large land mass at the beginning of Creation, but became separated during a major cataclysm. Some scholars speculate the division of the continents may have occurred during Noah's Flood. Genesis 7 and 8 indicate that it rained continuously for 40 days and nights (Genesis 7:12).

The inspired writer also notes that the "fountains of the great deep were opened" (Genesis 7:11), causing water to gush from underground springs, rivers and caverns, thus creating destruction and death over the entire planet. This event could have caused a major separation in the land, dropping some areas downward and pushing up mountains in other areas.

Another clue to the possible timing of such an event is found in Genesis 10. This scripture speaks of Shem's grandson, Peleg, and indicates that "in his day was the earth divided" (Genesis 10:25). Peleg's name can mean division, but it can also mean "earthquake." Some believe his name alludes to a physical division of the continents.

> [Peleg] from *paalag*—"to divide" because in his days, which is supposed to be about 100 years after the flood, the earth was divided among the sons of Noah. Though some are of the opinion that a physical division, and not a political one, is what is intended here, viz., a separation of continents and islands from the main land, the earthy parts having been united into one great continent previously to the days of Peleg. This

> opinion appears to me the most likely, for what is said in Genesis 10:5 is spoken by way of anticipation (comment on Genesis 10:25 in *The Adam Clarke Commentary*).

To speculate when this division of the land into separate continents occurred is not as important as the fact that this physical separation caused the continents to be lying on tectonic plates. Tectonic plates are slabs of rock between 50 to 650-feet thick. The plates carry the earth's continents and seas on an underground ocean of much hotter, semi-solid material.

The danger comes when a major volcanic eruption or an earthquake occurs, especially under the water. If the pressure under the sea is strong enough, it can create a shifting in the plates that produces not only a major earthquake, but in turn creates a deadly tsunami. A tsunami is a series of great sea waves. While they can be triggered by landslides or volcanic eruptions, most tsunamis originate as a result of underwater earthquakes.

Tsunamis are primarily generated by earthquakes in subduction zones. In these zones one section of the earth's crust, called a tectonic plate, moves over or under another. A giant rupture causes the seafloor to warp, displacing a vast amount of seawater. This raises the sea level and sets off the tsunami.

The devastation in December 2004, was created when the India and Burma plates collided, causing the tsunami to form. Billions of tons of water pounded the shores of 14 nations in a matter of hours! The collision of the plates produced:

- A 9.0 magnitude earthquake which was the strongest in 40 years

- Waves as high as 35 feet
- Waves traveling between 400 to 500 miles per hour
- Waves that caused death 3,200 miles away on the coast of Africa
- The deaths of more than 200,000 people, over a third of them children.

Geologists and seismologists indicate that the 9.0 quake was the fourth largest since 1899 when records were first kept. It was the fifth worst in world history. Just as in the days of Noah's flood, the people "knew not until the flood came and took them all away" (Matthew 24:39).

EARTHQUAKES AND THE LAST DAYS

For many years, ministers have pointed out that Jesus warned of future earthquakes in Matthew 24. The disciples of Christ had asked Him, "What will be the sign of Your coming and of the end of the age?" (Matthew 24:3). Jesus responded that one of the signs would be "earthquakes in various places" (Matthew 24:7).

I have pointed out that there have always been earthquakes of various magnitudes for centuries. However, there has been a massive increase in the number of quakes, the variety of their locations and the intensity of their strength, in our generation!

For example, in 1947, 1948, and 1949, there were only three major earthquakes during this prophetic time-frame when Israel was re-birthed as a nation. In the year 2004 there were thousands of quakes that rocked the land masses from one end of the earth to the other. Many people are familiar with land earthquakes but unfamiliar with underwater quakes. Even Jesus experienced sudden storms, and on one occasion during an underwater quake at the Sea of Galilee, Christ and his disciples were in a row boat crossing a section of the lake about four to six miles wide, when suddenly a storm struck the water.

> And a great windstorm arose, and the waves beat into the boat, so that it was already filling (Mark 4:37, 38).

Mark used the Greek *lailpas,* meaning a "squall, tempest, or storm." Matthew calls the storm a "great tempest" (Matthew 8:24). He uses a different Greek word, *seismos,* to describe the storm. The word alludes to an "underwater earthquake." Numerous underground hot springs bubble under the edges of the Sea of Galilee, and on this occasion there was a shaking under the water, producing huge waves that were covering the boat! Common Galilee storms are created by winds rushing across the rugged mountains surrounding the lake.

Matthew says this storm was created by a shaking in the bottom of the lake. When we say the word *seismograph,* we hear the Greek word *seismos* in it. The entire Galilee area in northern Israel was formed by ancient volcanic eruptions. Touring Israel today, one can observe the large dark volcanic stones littering the landscape throughout the upper Golan Heights. Today, the Sea of Galilee is approximately seven miles long by six miles wide. Evening storms caused by wind produce waves three to four feet high.

On this occasion in Christ's ministry, the tempest was formed by a mini underwater earthquake. Powerful and destructive tsunamis like the one recently experienced are also caused by massive underwater earthquakes, volcanic eruptions or the shifting of tectonic plates.

THE ENTIRE EARTH SHOOK

Scientists frightened many people when they announced that when this 9.0 underwater quake occurred, the entire earth shook. Some speculated that there was a slight shifting in the rotation of the earth. One news commentator announced it was a disaster of "Biblical proportions."

The gentleman may have been speaking prophetically without realizing it. The Bible predicts a time when the entire earth is going to shake violently. At one time this verse was considered the wild imagination of an overzealous Hebrew prophet. Isaiah prophecied about the future of the planet,

> The earth is violently broken, the earth is split open, the earth is shaken exceedingly. The earth shall reel to and fro like a drunkard, and shall totter like a hut (Isaiah 24:19, 20).

The prophet Haggai also saw a mighty shaking of the earth and the sea:

> For thus says the Lord of hosts: "Once more (it is a little while) I will shake heaven and earth, the sea and dry land; and I will shake all nations" (Haggai 2:6, 7).

These prophecies, once considered impossible, now seem not only possible, but probable. Scientists are saying that the tsunami forged a 600-mile-long crack at the bottom of the ocean, literally causing a split at the bottom of the sea. The 9.0 quake caused the entire earth to be moved and the impact was so powerful that the earth actually shifted slightly on its axis.

Prophetically, the Asian tsunami was another birth pain from Matthew 24:

> For nation will rise against nation, and kingdom against kingdom. And there will be famines, pestilences, and earthquakes in various places. All these are the beginning of sorrows (Matthew 24:7, 8).

The word *sorrows* is an old English word used when a pregnant woman went into labor pains. As she began to feel the intensity of the birthing pains, it was said she was entering the time of her sorrows. The Greek word Matthew used is *odin*, which can mean a time of grieving, but also means "birth pains." Just as believers will enter a time of travail before Christ's return, so the earth itself will enter its own time of birth pains which will be manifested through famines, pestilences and earthquakes. In Romans 8:22,Paul identified this time as the time when creation itself travails:

> For we know that the whole creation groans and labors with birth pangs together until now.

The Scriptures, the early church fathers and contemporary scholars have identified a time in the future as the Great Tribulation (Matthew 24:21; Mark 13:34; Revelation 7:14). This period of intense trouble will stretch over a seven-year period and will impact the earth and its inhabitants. Revelation describes events that would make a remarkable Hollywood science-fiction movie—with trees and grass burning, portions of the water becoming undrinkable and the sun scorching men (Revelation 8:7, 8:10-11 and 16:8). As these horrifying disasters grip the earth, the author reveals how men will react to such massive destruction leveling them from every side.

> And the kings of the earth, and the great men, and the rich men, and the commanders, the mighty men,

> and every slave and every free man, hid themselves in the caves and in the rocks of the mountains (Revelation 6:15).

This prediction, penned in 95 A.D. parallels a prophecy given to Isaiah 700 years prior to the vision of John in Revelation.

> They shall go into the holes of the rocks, and into the caves of the earth, from the terror of the Lord and the glory of His majesty. When He arises to shake the earth mightily (Isaiah 2:19).

The rocks (or caves) are found in the mountains; dens may be special, underground hiding chambers prepared by world governments for their leaders. In the mountains of Virginia there are several underground complexes where the President and his cabinet could be taken in the event of a major nuclear disaster. These underground structures are self-contained, and people could survive there for months and years.

Several years ago, news of a special bunker for the U.S. Congress was leaked by a journalist. The Cathedral of Praise in Ohio gave my family a special gift some time back—a three night stay at the Greenbrier Resort in White Sulfur Springs, West Virginia. Many presidents have stayed there.

At the height of the Cold War, the government secretly built an underground bunker next to this hotel for Congress to use in case of a nuclear attack. It was so secretive that only people directly connected with the building of the bunker, or those who guarded it, were aware of it and were sworn to secrecy.

Men who repaired the television sets in the hotel were actually secret government officials who oversaw the care of the bunker. It could only be entered by opening a huge wall inside the television repair shop, located in a room just off the convention center. The convention center, actually a part of the bunker, had two auditoriums that could serve as the meeting place for the House and the Senate in the event of a nuclear attack.

My son and I toured the bunker during our stay. We entered it from a huge concrete door which appeared to be an entrance to an underground power plant. I was shocked to see how the large complex had its own water filtering system, storage areas for food, bunk beds and meeting rooms, along with a hospital. There was also an incinerator to burn the garbage and to burn a human body in case a person died and they were unable to go outside for a burial.

This secret bunker was "discovered" in the early 1990s when a reporter was investigating a company that made safes. He noticed an old bill to the Greenbrier Hotel for several massive iron doors and wondered what a hotel would need with doors so massive. His investigation led the hotel to admit that the place existed. Those who had worked at the hotel for 20-30 years were amazed. None of them I spoke with had ever heard a discussion or had ever known that the large complex was right where they had been working.

Most governments have underground hideaways for their leaders in the event of a massive attack with unconventional weapons. Many of the secret bunkers are located in large mountains. The Bible indicates the "kings will run to the dens" (Revelation 6:15). The Greek word here can mean a *cavern*, a *hiding place* or a *resort.* As the earth shakes, kings and rich men will head to their "dens," and the common man will head to the mountains or the caves. I believe the mountains will be perceived as safer than the lowland areas or the coastal regions. Living in a cave will become so depressing, however, that men will ask God to allow the rocks to fall on them (Revelation 6:16).

THE BIG ONE IS COMING TO AMERICA

For years those living in California have been told to prepare for the "Big One." Geologists are speaking of a large earthquake that could occur at any time. The main fault line in California is the San Andreas Fault. This fault consists of two plates running through California: the Pacific plate on the west and the North American plate on the east.

It is more than 800 miles long and reaches at least 10 miles deep into the earth. The prediction is that eventually the plates will shift, causing one of the largest earthquakes in American history. The advantage in California is that large buildings are built and prepared to withstand strong earthquakes.

Few people on the east coast are aware that one of the largest fault lines in America is the New Madrid fault line. It lies within the central Mississippi Valley and extends from northeast Arkansas into southeast Missouri, western Tennessee, Kentucky, and into southern Illinois. The New Madrid area registers an average of 200 small tremors a year. A major quake in this area is considered more dangerous than the San Andreas area, since the ground in the New Madrid area would make a quake more widespread.

One of the last two major quakes along the New Madrid fault was in 1811-1812, when three quakes, estimated to have been larger than 8.0, struck in a three-month period. The second event was in 1895 when a 6.8 earthquake in New

Madrid was so strong that church bells rang in Boston! Both the Ohio and Mississippi Rivers "ran backwards!"

One of the most devastating quakes came to California in 1906. Its epicenter was San Francisco. Browsing through an antique store in Lake City, Tennessee, I came across an old book documenting the San Francisco quake. The earthquake struck on April 18, 1906 at 5:13 a.m. Fire burned and crumbled buildings for four-and-a-half square miles, leaving over 200,000 homeless.The recently revised death toll stands at 3,000.

This book, which was the property of a public school library in the 1940s, stated that most Americans believed the earthquake was a sign of God's judgment on the city for its wickedness! If a Bible believer made this same statement on a national news program today, he would be cut to shreds with verbal criticism and made a public mockery for saying God would judge anyone in such a manner. Even most Christians would act smug toward the notion.

America's gospel of prosperity and bless-me-now-if-you-can has created a lopsided understanding of God. We know His blessing but not His judgment. As the Bible states:

> I said, "Surely these are poor. They are foolish; for they do not know the way of the Lord, the judgment of their God (Jeremiah 5:4).

We must examine the scriptures in light of events, and discern the reason God allows or initiates certain events. It is interesting to note that the first record of a shaking of the earth that took the lives of people was when Korah rebelled against Moses (Numbers 16). In this instance, the earth opened up, and Korah and his house fell alive into the opening in the ground. The first shaking of the earth that took lives was over a rebellion against God's authority! Future shakings will come because of man's rebellion against God.

FUTURE SHAKINGS

In Revelation, John predicted the most devastating earthquake that is to occur in world history! It will happen during the latter part of a 7-year time known in prophecy as the Great Tribulation (Matthew 24:21, Revelation 7:14).

> And there were noises and thunderings and lightnings; and there was a great earthquake, such a mighty and great earthquake as had not occurred since men were on the earth (Revelation 16:18).

Great in the Greek text is *megas* and means "exceeding great." This earthquake will be so massive and intense that it will cause the entire planet to reel on its axis. Such an earthquake will cause a great change in the climate, impacting the poles. The results of such a dramatic shifting may be indirectly alluded to in this prophecy. After this massive global earthquake, huge hailstones will pound the planet and its inhabitants:

> And great hail from heaven fell upon men, each hailstone about the weight of a talent. Men blasphemed God because of the plague of the hail, since that plague was exceedingly great (Revelation 16:21).

Any major shifting in the polar ice caps would create a change in the earth's climate, producing massive flooding, earthquakes and huge chunks of ice falling from the sky in the form of hail. The hail in the Bible weighs a talent. A Jewish "talent" would equal about 113 pounds!

113 pds

Earth Reels Like a Drunkard

Such violent natural disasters could create an impact on earth similar to what the prophet Isaiah prophesied. He described how the Lord will "punish the [proud] ones and the kings of the earth" (v. 21).

> Behold, the Lord makes the earth empty and makes it waste, and distorts its surface and scatters abroad its inhabitants. Therefore the curse has devoured the earth, and those who dwell in it are desolate, therefore the inhabitants of the earth are burned, and few men are left.
>
> For the windows from on high are open, and the foundations of the earth are shaken. The earth is violently broken, the earth is split open, the earth is shaken exceedingly. The earth shall reel to and fro like a drunkard, and shall totter like a hut; its transgression shall be heavy upon it, and it will fall, and not rise again (Isaiah 24:1, 6, 18- 20).

What is interesting about this prophecy is that Isaiah said, "They shall cry aloud from the sea" (v. 14). He revealed how the Lord would be exalted "in the coastlands of the sea" (v. 15). We must consider the possibility that this prophecy could be fulfilled by a series of violent tsunamis occurring in the oceans of the world and affecting the coastlands of many nations.

The 2004 earthquake off the coast of Sumatra may have occurred five miles under the ocean, but it was equal to the power of a million atomic bombs, according to Kerry Sieh of the California Institute of Technology.

Richard Gross, a geophysicist with NASA's Jet Propulsion Laboratory in California, said it may have made the earth wobble. He said it appeared the massive quake caused the earth to spin three microseconds, or three millionths of a second, faster, and tilt about an inch on its axis. He also said this slight change was unlikely to cause any long-term effects.

Aother strange effect of such a large quake is that it could actually cause the day to be shortened. According to scientists, such a quake in the area of these tectonic plates could cause the earth's rotation to be changed. This would eventually shorten the day by a small margin. If a major slab slid down in the earth's core, the earth's rotation would slightly increase. If it were pushed away, the opposite would occur.

In light of these possibilities and in light of the fact that more tsunamis are expected in the future, it becomes clearer how certain unusual prophecies COULD be fulfilled.

Shortening the Days

The time of the Great Tribulation will be so terrible that Jesus warned:

> And unless those days were shortened, no flesh would be saved; but for the elect's sake those days will be shortened (Matthew 24:22).

This passage has been debated for centuries. If the time of Tribulation has already been set, then how could the days be shortened? A normal day is 24 hours and a normal solar year is 365.25 days. How does one "shorten the days?"

In Revelation, John tells us that the Tribulation will be two 42-month periods (Revelation 11:2; 13:5). John further explained how these two periods of 42 months each were divided into 1,260 days and 1,260 days (Revelation 11:3; 12:6).

A normal solar year has 365.25 days; however, the length of the Tribulation is calculated as 360 days making a year. Why is each year shortened by slightly over five days?

One explanation is that God's original calendar is a 360-day year, not a 365.25-day solar year. Therefore, if God is using His prophetic time compared to our present solar time, there would be a difference of about 35 days.

Comparing the Calendars	
Solar Calendar	**Prophetic Calendar**
365.25 days a year	360 days a year
7 years = 2,556.75 days	7 year tribulation = 2,520 days

The prophetic calendar is 36.25 days shorter than the solar calendar. Therefore, the time of the Tribulation would be "shortened" by slightly over 36 days, using God's calendar of 360 days making a year.

Another possible explanation could involve future tsunamis and earthquakes that could change the rotation of the earth and literally shorten the days. It is difficult to definitely say that this is how this strange prophecy will come to pass. When the Hebrew prophets foresaw the earth reeling and shaking like a drunk, with massive numbers of casualties and deaths, we can now see how these unusual predictions could come to pass in our time. A massive shifting of the tectonic plates under the sea would cause:

- An earthquake, which would knock down buildings
- A massive tsunami, bringing walls of water to the coastlines

- A shaking of the planet, changing the rotation of the earth

When Isaiah saw the earth being shaken, he also mentioned the cry of the sea and the coastlands. Again, the prophetic word identifies the sea and the coastlines as places of future trouble. Several of the future Biblical judgments that will impact the sea and the marine life are recorded in Revelation. Prophecy tells of a huge meteorite set to strike the earth during the future Tribulation:

> Then the third angel sounded: And a great star fell from heaven, burning like a torch, and it fell on a third of the rivers and on the springs of water. The name of the star is Wormwood. A third of the waters became wormwood, and many men died from the water, because it was made bitter (Revelation 8:10, 11).

John saw a burning star fall from heaven and strike the earth. This no doubt alludes to a large meteorite hitting a certain section of the earth. The meteorite will be named *wormwood*. This falling star will affect the drinking water making a third of the rivers and springs of water bitter, and even causing death in a third of the world.

If a large meteorite impacted any ocean of the world, it would produce huge tidal waves, bringing gigantic walls of water crashing over the coastlines of the continents. Most scientists speculate that dinosaurs were wiped out by a major event such as a meteorite. With the combination of volcanic eruptions, underwater earthquakes and falling stars, one can easily see how these strange prophecies concerning the judgments of God during the 7-year Tribulation can literally come to pass.

On several occasions, large meteorites have passed the earth. Many scientists fear that in the future a large falling star could hit the planet, causing untold damage and disaster to the earth, along with millions of lives lost. As the birth pains and early signs of the times begin to come to pass, these events will cause a major shaking of the nations. This phenomenon was predicted by inspired men of God in the Holy Scriptures.

Once more (it is a little while) I will shake heaven and earth, the sea and dry land; and I will shake all nations . . . they shall come to the Desire of All Nations . . . and I will fill this temple with glory," says the Lord of hosts (Haggai 2:6, 7).

2

The Shaking of the Nations

Not until the tsunami struck had I ever taken a close look at the number of passages where the Hebrew prophets warned the kings of Babylon, Egypt, Tyre and Lebanon of coming judgment. These prophecies were identified as the "shaking of the nations" by several of the Hebrew prophets (Ezekiel 31:16; Haggai 2:7).

In Haggai's prophecy, the man of God lists four things that will experience this future shaking from God:

- The heavens will be shaken.
- The earth will be shaken.
- The sea will be shaken.
- The dry land will be shaken.

The Hebrew word for "shake" in Haggai, *ra'ash*, is translated in the Kings James Bible as "move," "quake," "shake," "tremble" and "to make afraid." Reviewing the prophecy of Haggai, one can see how these predictions will come to pass. The earth will be shaken through major shifting in the earth's underwater plates. The sea will be shaken though a tsunami or a major storm on the sea. The shaking of dry land alludes to a major earthquake. The heavens shaking, no doubt, refers to the many predictions that large stars (meteorites) will fall from heaven and strike the earth.

These prophetic shakings are clearly visible throughout the Book of Revelation during the 7-year Great Tribulation.

> **1. The shaking of the heavens.** And the stars of heaven fell to the earth, as a fig tree drops its late figs when it is shaken by a mighty wind. Then the sky receded as a scroll when it is rolled up, and every mountain and island was moved out of its place (Revelation 6:13, 14).
>
> **2. The shaking of the earth and dry land.** And there were noises and thunderings and lightnings; and there was a great earthquake, such a mighty and great earthquake as had not occurred since men were on the earth. Then every island fled away, and the mountains were not found (Revelation 16:18, 20).
>
> **3. The shaking of the sea.** Then the second angel poured out his bowl on the sea, and it became blood as of a dead man; and every living creature in the sea died (Revelation 16:3).

These scriptures identify judgments released by angels during the Tribulation. Those living on earth will view these judgments as natural disasters, but those in heaven understand they are the judgments of God. These sins include the shedding of innocent blood, fornication, worshiping idols and persecuting the righteous. These destructive acts will have a great impact on the shipping industry and commerce throughout the world (Revelation 18:17-24).

THE OLD TESTAMENT PATTERNS

In Old Testament times, the world's leading commercial and sea powers were Babylon, Assyria, Lebanon and Egypt. These nations built ships and used seaports to distribute goods across the Mediterranean, the Nile region, and the Euphrates and Tigris River valley. They had contact with merchants from other nations, and most had a thriving fishing industry. Imports and exports helped build wealth in these nations.

A major judgment against these nations always impacted their economy in a negative manner. Whenever the fishing industry was ruined, fishermen were left without an income. When the ports were destroyed, the merchantmen and ship owners were left without means to create income or receive and distribute goods.

Ezekiel gave a prophetic word against the King of Tyre (Lebanon) in Ezekiel 26. God warned the inhabitants of the city that the Babylonians would invade them. The Almighty said, "I am against you, O Tyre, and will cause many nations to come up against you, as the sea causes its waves to come up" (Ezekiel 26:3). The reaction of the surrounding nations to Tyre's destruction is recorded by Ezekiel:

> Thus says the Lord God to Tyre: "Will the coastlands not shake at the sound of your fall, when the

> wounded cry, when slaughter is made in the midst of you? Then all the princes of the sea will come down from their thrones, lay aside their robes, and take off their embroidered garments; they will clothe themselves with trembling; they will sit on the ground, tremble every moment, and be astonished at you. And they will take up a lamentation for you (Ezekiel 26:15-17).

During early times in ancient Israel, the Philistines were a large tribe settled along the coastal areas of Israel. They inhabited five major cities with strong connections to all the major shipping ports on the Mediterranean Sea. When God was preparing judgment for this people, the Philistines, the prophet Ezedkel warned them of the destruction of their seacoast:

> Thus says the Lord God: "I will stretch out My hand against the Philistines, and I will cut off the Cherethites and destroy the remnant of the seacoast. I will execute great vengeance on them with furious rebukes; and they shall know that I am the Lord, when I lay My vengeance upon them" (Ezekiel 25:16, 17).

Millions of people from countless tribes and nations live in the coastlands, on islands and near oceans or large seas. The Mediterranean Sea is the water bridge connecting northern Africa, Israel, Lebanon, parts of Asia, and Europe. America has the Atlantic and the Pacific Oceans.

A future tsunami, volcanic eruption or earthquake can and will affect the coastlines and the populations living near them. This will create tragedies of Biblical proportions.

A WARNING TO THE NATIONS

When a major event occurs (a global war, devastating earthquake or some other major disaster) it raises questions: *Was this from God or from Satan, or was it just a bizarre natural disaster?*

This is a politically correct time in America. We don't want to offend someone whose beliefs may differ from ours. This often weakens preaching from the pulpits and tends to motivate ministers to emphasize only the positive. They tend to be overly optimistic about the future, even when warnings of future judgment are clear from prophetic scriptures. Ministers often appear to be "dueling prophets"—one warning of the trouble to come and another rejecting the warning and predicting great prosperity in spite of man's wickedness.

Despite self-inspired, positive prophecies, the wrath of God's judgment will eventually be poured out on Gentile nations. Can an event that takes hundreds of thousands of lives be classified as an act of God? Is it a warning to idol-worshiping nations to search out the Creator of mankind and the Savior of the world, Jesus Christ? The phrase "judgment of God" creates different images and concepts to those who hear it. Just what is the Biblical definition of God's judgment?

DEFINING THE JUDGMENT OF GOD

The common Hebrew word in the Old Testament for "judgment" is *mishpat,* meaning "passing a verdict, either favorable or unfavorable." It alludes to God's passing sentence on situations involving His people. When we speak of God sending judgment to a nation, He is sending a judgment based on evidence against the nation.

An Old Testament example was God's judgment against Sodom and Gomorrah. Prior to its destruction, the Lord informed Abraham of His plans (Genesis 18:17-21). Abraham requested the cities be spared if 10 righteous people could be found, and the Lord agreed.

Then God sent two angels (two witnesses) into the city to verify that the wickedness was great. Not only could they not find 10 righteous, but the men of the city rose up and attempted to physically seduce the two angels who had appeared in the form of two men (Genesis 19:5). Only four righteous people were found, therefore the cities were destroyed once the righteous were gone from the area.

Ezekiel revealed the major sins that caused God's wrath to be unleashed on those cities. The sins included pride, fullness of bread, abundance of idleness, not caring for the needy and of course, the abomination of same-sex relationships (Ezekiel 16:49, 50). Once the verdict was given, destruction came suddenly and unexpectedly to the cities.

In the New Testament the word *judgment* is used in several ways. A *judgment hall* was where religious leaders and the High Priest met to determine legal action. This was where Christ stood trial (John 18:28). Another word for *judgment* refers to the heavenly judgment of the righteous and the unrighteous. The righteous will receive rewards at the judgment seat of Christ, *bema* (Romans 14:10-14), and the unrighteous and sinners will stand before the Great White Throne Judgment as predicted in Revelation 20:11-15.

Another meaning of *judgment* in the New Testament is the ability to correctly discern, or to have perception in a matter (Philippians 1:9). In 1 Corinthians 7:25, Paul speaks of giving his "judgment" concerning virgins marrying in the church.

The Greek word in this passage means "to give an
based on information." One remaining word for *judgment* in the New Testament is the Greek word *krima*, which means to condemn something in a court of law, or to make a decision against a crime which was committed.

In America our local, regional and nationally elected leaders have passed laws protecting individuals and their property. When these laws are broken, punishment is pronounced on the guilty party. This punishment may involve doing some type of community service time, or the restitution of money or goods. In many cases, it involves varying degrees of incarceration. If a person is found guilty of murder, he often faces life in prison or the death penalty.

We don't think twice if the judicial system condemns a mass murderer to die, but many have difficulty understanding why God permits His judgment to come upon rebellious and ungodly nations whose sins infect the population like contagious gangrene.

How Is Judgment Revealed?

God is the creator of all elements, including earth, wind, fire and water. The earth rotates at the proper speed and is positioned in the heavens at the perfect distance from the sun. This prevents humans from being scorched by the sun or frozen to death by being positioned too far from the sun. The rain falls in proper seasons and the waves of the ocean beat against the shore about 26 times per minute.

It is amazing how gravity holds things down, and how the earth can rotate so fast without falling apart. This is because God is "upholding all things by the word of His power" (Hebrews 1:3).

When God decides to judge His creation, he often allows four main elements of creation to manifest His wrath. These elements are listed, with an example of the form they take.

Element	Manifestation	Example
The Water	Floods, Tsunamis	Genesis 7, 8
The Fire	Volcanoes, Fires	Genesis 19
The Wind	Hurricanes/Tornados	Genesis 11*
The Earth	Earthquakes	Numbers 16

* (A Jewish tradition holds that a strong and mighty wind blew down the tower.)

The devastation caused by these "natural" elements can be seen by looking at the three geographical divisions of the United Sates. Each division is occasionally impacted by one or two of the above natural elements. For example:

- The west coast is under the continuous threat of earthquakes and strange fires breaking out in the high mountains during the dry seasons.
- The central U.S. is often hit with tornadoes, flooding and, at times, terrible droughts.
- The east coast gets slammed with hurricanes.

These elements may hit a small town or several communities during any 12-month period. When a disaster impacts the entire nation and its damage and destruction are beyond normal limits, then we must ask ourselves if there is a divine link to what has happened.

As believers, we know that if God judged the cities of Sodom and Gomorrah and judged Jerusalem and Israel for dishonoring

His Word and breaking His commandments, then America and other nations of the world are in line for our own seasons of trouble unless there is a massive repentance and turning to God.

What Is Holding Back the Judgment of God?

What is restraining a sudden manifestation of God's judgment? Countless countries are filled with idolatry, adultery, fornication, the shedding of innocent blood and the persecution of dedicated Christians. Should God allow nations to continue mocking His people and His Word, and permit them to deceive the masses into worshiping dead religious idols who can't even feed themselves or speak?

It is clear from the story of Lot that the presence of righteous and godly people is a restraint against God's judgment. When Lot fled Sodom, he requested to move to a small city in the mountains called Zoar. This city is one of five that should have been destroyed, but Lot's presence caused the angel to restrain judgment on this small community.

The presence of a righteous man helped hold back a planned judgment against Zoar (Genesis 19:17-23). This is why some scholars believe that born-again believers will be taken to heaven prior to the 7-year Tribulation. Even the angels in Lot's day could not release fire on Sodom and Gomorrah until Lot was safe in Zoar!

> [The angel] said to [Lot], "See, I have favored you concerning this thing also, in that I will not overthrow this city for which you have spoken. Hurry, escape there. For I cannot do anything until you arrive there" (Genesis 19:21, 22).

The apostle Paul mentioned a restrainer keeping the man of sin (the Antichrist) from being revealed (2 Thessalonians 2). The apostle Peter taught that the heavens and earth are being kept in store, "reserved for fire until the day of judgment and perdition of ungodly men" (2 Peter 3:7). We are living in a time when God is restraining judgment that could come at any moment. He is patient and longsuffering toward humanity. As the apostle Peter said, God is "not willing that any should perish but that all should come to repentance" (2 Peter 3:9).

When man's cup of iniquity is full and humankind has crossed the line of God's patience, then God's wrath will be released across the entire planet, thus creating the final Tribulation. The ultimate time of God's wrath and judgment on sinful nations is being reserved for the seven years of Tribulation.

Between now and then the world will see and experience periods of selective judgment and intense birth pangs as we approach the time of Christ's return. When a major labor pain impacts this planet, we must not think the Great Tribulation has arrived. These events are only precursors of coming prophetic events. They are signs, however, of birth pangs, or the "beginning of sorrows" (Matthew 24:7, 8). The closer we move to the return of Christ, the more common, the more frequent and the more intense the birth pangs will become.

The Nations and the Tsunami

The size of the land mass that felt the impact of the tsunami was equal to the size of the United States! Twelve nations and the small islands of the Seychelles felt various levels of impact from the 2004 tsunami. In the Bible, numbers are significant and often carry a prophetic meaning.

For example, in the Scriptures the number three always alludes to unity; the number six is the number for man, and the number seven is completion. Twelve is a number for government and divine order. The 12 sons of Jacob formed a nation called Israel. Twelve disciples formed the nucleus of the original church. Revelation 5 tells of 24 elders, or 12 multiplied twice.

In any disaster with global repercussions there is usually a prophetic parallel that can be discerned from the Scripture. After the tsunami struck the coastlines of these nations, I began to question, "What do the nations which suffered the most loss have in common?"—other than they are all in the Pacific Rim and are considered a part of Asia? A month after the tsunami, the 12 main nations affected reported:

Nation	Population	Death Toll
Indonesia	228,437,870	237,071
Sri Lanka	19,905,165	30,957
India	1,029,991,145	16,389
Thailand	61,797,751	5,393
Somalia	8,304,601	298
Maldives	310,764	108
Myanmar	48,000,000	90
Malaysia	22,229,040	74
Tanzania	36,588,225	10
Bangladesh	131,269,860	2
South Africa	36,588,225	2
Kenya	32,021,856	1

In addition, 3,071 people are listed as missing in Thailand and 5,637 in Sri Lanka, but will not be counted in the death toll until they are missing for a year. (The small islands of the Seychelles had three deaths). Among the three main nations where the destruction and loss of lives was greatest—Indonesia, India and Sri Lanka—their religious beliefs represent three non-Christian religions of the world. The major religions of these three countries are:

Country	**Religion**
Indonesia	95 percent Muslim
India	81 percent Hindu
Sri Lanka	70 percent Buddhist

Each of these three nations has a remnant of Christians who are attempting to practice their faith under great persecution and often under life-threatening situations. Each country has one main thing in common as it relates to Christianity—all three have persecuted, beaten and, at times, killed Christians. They have also burned down or shut down numerous Christian churches.

In Indonesia, there are pockets of so-called "jihadists." Missionary friends have been stopped by men waving red flags and wearing red bandanas who force cars to stop and give a financial donation to Islam. In all three countries, churches are under some form of government pressure and continual threat. They could be bombed during a service or have their building burned during the night.

Larger Christian churches that can afford it often have bomb squads with bomb-sniffing dogs to sweep their buildings before services begin. Over 600 Christian churches have been burned to the ground. Thousands of practicing Christians have no building in which to meet because their structure was burned by Islamic fanatics.

Fanatical Hindus have been persecuting Christians and burning churches in India for years. A missionary and his two sons were burned alive in their vehicle a few years ago. Many Indians want a completely Hindu nation, and want to ban all other religions. A missionary friend has been banned from India. The government there told him he was making too many Christian converts.

India recently passed laws limiting evangelism. Hindi fanatics continually harass and persecute anyone whose beliefs are opposite their own. Perhaps the most striking story of the tsunami occurred on the small island of Sri Lanka, just off the southeastern point of India.

In December 2003, two Buddhist monks began a campaign to persecute Christians there. An American missionary called a fast, then prophesied that God was going to judge the two men. The next day one of the men dropped dead, and the following day, the other monk died suddenly. This infuriated the other Buddhist leaders, and they came after the American and began a campaign of persecution on Christmas Day, 2003.

This was exactly one year before the tsunami struck their island!

In December 2004, three weeks before the tsunami devastated the Sri Lanka coastline, the largest Catholic church in the nation was burned to the ground by Buddhist fanatics. The reason this is significant is that God gave warnings about persecuting and killing the righteous. He warned that those engaged in this activity would "drink of the wine of the wrath of God" (Revelation 14:10). Twice God's wrath is said to be placed in a cup: a "cup of His indignation" (Revelation 14:10), and the "cup of the wine of the fierceness of His wrath" (Revelation 16:19).

> For thus says the Lord God of Israel to me: "Take this wine cup of fury from My hand, and cause all the nations, to whom I send you, to drink it. And they will drink and stagger and go mad because of the sword that I will send among them" (Jeremiah 25:15, 16).

Ezekiel also speaks of the cup that God gives, which ungodly men must drink. He explained that idol worship is one of the primary reasons that God's anger is poured out.

> I will do these things to you because you have gone as a harlot after the Gentiles, because you have become defiled by their idols. You have walked in the way of your sister; therefore I will put her cup in your hand (Ezekiel 23:30, 31).

One reason for these violent judgments during the Tribulation is that the nations have shed the blood of righteous men and women. They persecute those who believe in and have accepted Jesus Christ. The individuals who are killed for the gospel are identified in Revelation:

> When He opened the fifth seal, I saw under the altar the souls of those who had been slain for the word of God and for the testimony which they held. And they cried with a loud voice, saying, "How long, O Lord, holy and true, until You judge and avenge our blood on those who dwell on the earth?" (Revelation 6:9, 10).

The wrath of God will strike the nations in the future because of the cry of innocent blood that has been shed on earth. The blood of millions of martyrs cries out from the dust to Almighty God. As men and women drink from the cup of

God's anger, they will literally be drinking from waters polluted by storms, volcanic eruptions and meteorites. The angel of the Lord explains the reason for this judgment:

> For they have shed the blood of saints and prophets, and you have given them blood to drink. For it is their just due (Revelation 16:6).

When God sees His covenant children slain by religious fanatics and persecuted by those who worship idols and false gods, the wrath of God is eventually released against those nations and individuals. This occurred in Egypt prior to the exodus of the Hebrews. Scholars note that when 10 plagues were sent from God against the Egyptians, there were 10 gods of the Egyptians that should have, but could not, stop the plagues. God's 10 acts of judgment were actually an attack on and a mockery against the helpless idol of the Egyptians.

ATTACKING THE IDOL GODS

Lest someone think this prophetic observation is the wild imagination of a Bible-thumping preacher, let us examine the parallel warnings God gave to ancient Israel and see how these same warnings and judgments are proactive today.

The only true God is the God of Abraham, Isaac and Jacob. His inspired Word was given to the Hebrew prophets who penned the words of the Bible. One feature that marks Scripture above other religious writings is the prophecy in the Bible. The Holy Spirit inspired the prophets to write about events that would transpire thousands of years later. Prophetic students and scholars note that when Bible prophecies come to pass, they occur with such pinpoint accuracy, that this alone would indicate the inspiration of the written Word.

Because there is only one true God, He despises idol worship. The utter foolishness of a man creating an image of wood, metal or stone and bowing before it is utterly useless. God often mocks idol worshippers in Scripture, just as Elijah mocked the false prophets of Baal who were unable to call fire down from heaven on their sacrifices (1 Kings 18).

Many of the Asian rim nations worship numerous false gods and idols. For example, India is 81 percent Hindu. The Hindu religion has millions of gods, one representing every living thing. The top three gods are Shiva, Ganesh and Vishnu. Different regions of India worship different types of gods.

Not far from where the tsunami struck in India, there is a rat temple where millions of rats are adored and worshiped. Thousands of locals bring food to the rats every morning and evening, believing they are appeasing the rat god. Although many families may experience a shortage of food, the rats are well fed every day. In Sri Lanka, not far from where the tsunami struck, there is a Buddhist temple which claims to have the tooth of the founder of Buddhism.

It is clear that nations like these have millions of people in spiritual darkness who believe their idols control all things. However, these gods were not able to provide protection from the disaster, and cannot heal their sick or provide needed food for relief.

Indonesia's main religion is Islam. Many Muslims in Indonesia are considered moderate, but many others want every vestige of the Christian faith removed from the Indonesian islands. Christians have lived under threats for years, and continue to do so. Muslims pray to Allah, which they teach is an Arabic form of God's name. Many scholars point out, however, that this name existed in the time of

Mohammad and is actually a name which identified a moon deity worshiped by many Arab tribes living then.

In the Bible, one of the major sins that God continually rebuked Israel and the nations for was the sin of idolatry. The Hebrew prophets often identified the root source of God's anger as His frustration with the nations for turning to a man-made object and calling it a god. When nations honored false gods, then those nations, including Israel, were sent a warning, followed by an act of judgment.

THREE SINS THAT BRING GOD'S JUDGMENT

Jeremiah screamed out his warnings to Israel prior to the Babylonian invasion. The ancient Hebrew prophet listed three main sins that removed God's favor and lifted God's hedge from Israel, thus opening the door to Israel's enemies to invade the land and capture the Jews and the Temple wealth.

1. They burned incense to other gods (Jeremiah 19:4).
2. They built high places of idol worship (Jeremiah 19:5).
3. They filled Jerusalem with innocent blood (Jeremiah 19:4).

Many nations on the Asian rim have large, ancient temples erected to various gods where they burn incense to their idols daily. In many of the mountainous regions, temples are erected on high places to be "closer" to the heavens. Innocent blood is shed when civil and religious wars take innocent lives and when many Christians lay down their lives for the gospel.

In Jeremiah God warned that judgment would come as a result of these sins. The passage creates an eerie feeling when it is compared with events linked to the tsunami.

> Thus says the Lord of hosts: "Behold, disaster shall go forth from nation to nation, and a great whirlwind shall be raised up from the farthest parts of the earth.
>
> "And at that day the slain of the Lord shall be from one end of the earth even to the other end of the earth. They shall not be lamented, or gathered, or buried; they shall become refuse on the ground" (Jeremiah 25:32, 33).

This is not a prophecy for Israel only. God said disaster will go from one nation to another. The King James Bible said the whirlwind will "come from the coasts of the earth." The Hebrew word *coasts* is used three times in Jeremiah (25:32; 31:8; 50:41), and means "the border," "the coasts," "the quarter side."

Jeremiah predicted the people slain would not be lamented, gathered or buried. It is impossible to conduct a normal, physical funeral for someone missing after a tsunami or who has drowned at sea. It is also impossible to gather together missing bodies. So many victims lay on the ground for days. It was the saddest and most moving sight I have seen in many years. The pictures aired around the world are similar to the prophetic warning from Jeremiah!

THE BIGGER QUESTION

If a person assumes that this terrible event was a divine warning to the idol worshiping, Christian-persecuting nations, then a most difficult question is, "Why did so many innocent people, including children, suffer?" Why the innocent and the children suffer brings a great division of opinions among theologians discussing disasters and tragedies. If we say the disaster was the wrath of God, then God is viewed by the rationalists as some angry, cosmic deity who gets pleasure out of innocent people suffering. If we believe the tragedy serves as a warning to the nations then the question arises, "Why didn't God take out just the idol worshipers, or the Christian-killers and some of their temples? Why did tourists and people who were visiting those nations encounter such a sudden tragedy?"

When Jeremiah was giving his warnings of impending disaster on Israel, he made a powerful statement: "And the peaceful dwellings are cut down because of the fierce anger of the Lord" (Jeremiah 25:37). When trouble strikes, good *and* bad people are often in the middle of the disaster.

1. Jesus taught that the heavenly Father "makes His sun rise on the evil and on the good, and sends rain on the just and on the unjust (Matthew 5:45, 46). As long as good and bad people live on the same planet, they will both experience trouble when it comes to an area. Just because a person is righteous does not exempt him from tragedy. Christians lose their homes in floods, hurricanes and tornadoes. The difference in the righteous and the unrighteous is that an unbeliever is left feeling hopeless, but believers can still maintain their faith in God and have peace in the midst of the storm.

2. People are in the wrong place at the wrong time on occasion. Through the years I have heard amazing stories of believers who were warned by the Holy Spirit not to take a journey or go to a certain place. They later learned that a terrorist act or a natural disaster had occurred, and they would have been in the center of the danger.

Others, who may not have been as sensitive to the Spirit, were in harm's way. We must learn to follow the inner nudging of the Holy Spirit who can "show you things to come" and even warn you of dangers that lie ahead (John 16:13; Acts 20:22-24).

3. God's blessings flowed through Israel as long as they followed His commandments. As the nations turned to idolatry, God sent famine, pestilence and the sword to mock the prayers to the idol gods. No idol could stop the Almighty's hand of wrath.

> You are wearied in the multitude of your counsels; Let now the astrologers, the stargazers, and the monthly prognosticators stand up and save you from what shall come upon you.
>
> Behold, they shall be as stubble, the fire shall burn them; they shall not deliver themselves from the power of the flame; it shall not be a coal to be warmed by, nor a fire to sit before! Thus shall they be to you with whom you have labored, your merchants from your youth; they shall wander each one to his quarter. No one shall save you (Isaiah 47:13-15).
>
> Assemble yourselves and come; draw near together, you who have escaped from the nations. They have no knowledge. Who carry the wood of their carved image, and pray to a god that cannot save (Isaiah 45:20).

Ironically, we expect wicked people to experience bad things and good people to always experience good things. When we heard that Saddam's sons were killed, many said, "They deserved what they got. The Lord's vengeance was upon them." However, when good people are killed, believers comment, "This should not have happened. What did they do to deserve this?"

Good or bad people experiencing trouble is not always linked to what a person deserves. Sometimes it simply rains on the just and the unjust. A natural disaster is sometimes the consequence of living on a cursed earth that is travailing and waiting to be delivered. At other times, warnings may have been ignored. Lot's sons-in-law and daughters mocked him when he warned them the city would be destroyed. They refused the warning and suffered along with the wicked in the city (Genesis 19:12-14).

WHAT ABOUT INNOCENT CHILDREN?

To those who believe and accept the Bible, it is understandable that God would permit a judgment to be made against murderers, idolaters, fornicators, liars, thieves and others. But it is difficult for both Christians and non-Christians to fathom why the Almighty permits small, innocent children to die at such an early age. Often people ask, "What have they done wrong to "deserve" this? This question has initiated heated debates between theologians, ministers and lay people, especially those raising a family.

First, consider the children who have died at the hands of wicked men and through false religious worship. In the days of the Pharaoh of Egypt, a decree was made that all male Hebrew children born to Hebrew mothers were to be drowned in the river by the Egyptian midwives (Exodus 1:22).

Inhabitants of ancient Jerusalem once worshiped an idol called Molech, an iron god that had the appearance of a cow from the waist up and a human from the waist down. An opening in its belly was heated with tar and wood. Children were passed through the fire of Molech to appease this idol (2 Kings 16:3; 17:17; 21:6; 23:10). Some scholars believe that infants were actually thrown into the burning belly of this Canaanite deity.

In the New Testament, Herod had all infants under two years slain by Roman soldiers in and around Bethlehem (Matthew 2:16). From early history, innocent children have suffered at the hands of wicked and cruel men. Time would fail to mention the children who died during history's wars, famines and pestilences. Imagine the innocent children who suffered both starvation and eventual death at the hands of the Nazis during the holocaust. Some estimate that 1.5 million victims of Hitler's holocaust were children!

JUDGMENT AND CHILDREN

When judgment came in Noah's day as the great flood, all mankind and animals were drowned in the murky, rushing waters, including infants and children. In Lot's day we have no recorded number of infants and children who may have been living with parents in the four burning cities. The same can be said of the Roman invasion of Jerusalem in the year 70 A.D., an event prophesied by Christ that wreaked total destruction on Jerusalem and the Temple (Matthew 24:2).

Knowing the destruction of Jerusalem and the future Great Tribulation would be so terrible, Jesus warned, "Woe to those who are pregnant and to those who are nursing babies in those days!" (Matthew 24:19). When children are affected by wars, famines, earthquakes, pestilences and other judgments, it moves our hearts.

This was true with the Pharaoh of Egypt. God sent nine plagues to destroy crops, cattle, the water and the land. Nothing moved Pharaoh until the 10th plague hit his home. He and all the Egyptians lost their firstborn sons to the angel of death (Exodus 12). Pharaoh lost a son who was heir to the throne. This judgment finally broke the stony heart of Egypt's dictator. The death of children often stirs more compassion and humility than anything else.

JESUS LOVES THE CHILDREN

It may seem like a contradiction to say that God allows judgment to come even when children are involved, and then talk about how much Jesus loves children! The Bible reveals that Christ had much to say about children. During His earthly ministry Christ spent time blessing children (Mark 10:13).

When the disciples attempted to stop children from seeking Jesus' attention, He rebuked them and said, "Let the little children come to Me, and do not forbid them; for of such is the kingdom of God" (Mark 10:14). Jesus also stated that whoever would receive a little child in his name was also receiving Him (Mark 9:37). On one occasion, Jesus said that angels watch over children:

> Take heed that you do not despise one of these little ones, for I say to you that in heaven their angels always see the face of My Father who is in heaven (Matthew 18:10).

If Christ loves children and angels are guarding their steps, then why are children starving in Africa, India and other third world nations. Why did so many children die in the Asian tsunami?

MERCY THROUGH DEATH

In Judaism there is a belief that a child is not responsible for his own sins until he reaches the age of 13. On the 13th birthday, religious Jews celebrate bar-mitzvah, a ceremony identifying the child as a young adult, now responsible for his own sins. Christians often speak of the "age of accountability," when a child is personally responsible for his own sins and for answering to God for his own choices. Many believe, as I do, that the age of accountability may vary, depending on the child's mental and spiritual maturity. However, age 12 or 13 seems to be an age where adolescence kicks in and the child enters a mental, spiritual and physical age of personal accountability and responsibility.

I and many others believe that prior to this age, if a child dies he goes to be with the Lord. One example is when King David's illegitimate child was stricken with an illness shortly after its birth. The king fasted seven days for the infant's recovery but in the end the child died. David said:

> But now he is dead; why should I fast? Can I bring him back again? I shall go to him, but he shall not return to me (2 Samuel 12:23).

David knew his child's soul and spirit had gone on to be with the Lord, and he could not raise the infant from the dead. He did realize, however, that one day he would die and his soul and spirit would join his son's.

Many children in the world live in terrible poverty, starvation and great distress. God allows death at times because He does not wish to see the little ones suffer any more. At death, their souls and spirits are carried by the angels to a place called paradise (Luke 16:22; 2 Corinthians 12:2-4).

Imagine the moment when they leave the hunger, pain and suffering of this life and are escorted into the third heaven, a paradise where the angels care for the soul and spirit! When small children die in third world countries, I call it mercy through death. Years ago, a missionary friend traveled to Africa, to the heart of a nation where famine and starvation were sweeping the bush like a deadly plague. He saw children whose physical bodies were simply skeletons with a layer of dark skin.

At first he questioned God: *Why did these people suffer*? He knew that the government was corrupt and evil. He knew that bribery, child abuse and false religion abounded in that place. He knew the leaders cared only for their own prosperity and allowed their people to suffer in an inexcusable way.

Then he realized that through natural death these children were freed from these terrible conditions and released into God' presence.

In Times of Judgment

If the Almighty initiates judgment on a nation or series of nations, children will inevitably be caught in the middle. Yet, consider what many face. They are being raised in poverty by a family who worships idols and gives their food to stone gods at some man-made temple.

In many countries, children are sexually molested by family members and friends, and forced to beg in the streets. In India, some parents will physically maim a child and make him a beggar on the streets.

If a child dies before the age of accountability, the Lord extends a special mercy for the soul of the innocent. When the child becomes an adult, however, and begins practicing idolatry, adultery, fornication and other ungodly things, that soul is responsible for his own actions and accountability. The death of the righteous and the innocent keep them from seeing the evil days which are coming:

> The righteous man perishes, and no one lays it to heart; and merciful and devout men are taken away, with no one considering that the uncompromisingly upright and godly person is taken away from the calamity and evil to come [even through wickedness] (Isaiah 57:1, *AMP*).

> The righteous pass away; the godly often die before their time. And no one seems to care or wonder why. No one seems to understand that God is protecting them from the evil to come (Isaiah 57:1, *NLT*).

When an innocent child passes, God could be sparing him from the trouble he could experience in the future. The book of Jasher says that the Lord takes the righteous away so they will not be grieved by the sin and wickedness that is coming to the earth. If Christ tarries we will all die, either by old age, a physical infirmity, an accident, or some form of disaster. The physical body is still subject to death.

And as it was in the days of Noah, so it will be also in the days of the Son of Man: they ate, they drank, they married wives, they were given in marriage, until the day that Noah entered the ark, and the flood came and destroyed them all (Luke 17:26, 27).

3

Parallels To the Days of Noah

The things which have been are the things which shall be (Ecclesiastes 1:9, 10). In other words, the future has already been revealed through incidents from the past. Jesus made it clear that the time of His return would be like two previous time periods in Biblical history—the days of Noah and the days of Lot.

These two periods of history are recorded in the Book of Genesis. The days of Noah were the times and seasons just before the universal flood. The days of Lot were the events which preceded the destruction of the cities of Sodom and Gomorrah. Christ gave us clues that these two time periods would parallel events just before His return. Ministers often point out the common link between our present society and the days of Noah and Lot, which are recorded in Luke 17:26-30. These parallel signs include:

- Eating
- Drinking
- Marrying
- Building
- Planting
- Selling
- Buying

After researching the Scriptures, I always felt there were more clues to the days of Noah and Lot than just the ones penned in the Gospel of Luke. The story of Noah and the flood is told in Genesis 6-9. The incident involving Lot and the destruction of Sodom and Gomorrah is recorded in Genesis 19. I began to carefully examine each verse in Genesis to see if other clues were evident, paralleling our day with these important historic accounts.

I observed two main elements linked to the times of Noah and Lot. In Noah's day the central feature was *water*, and in Lot's day the central feature of the story was *fire* and *brimstone.* How does rain and fire and brimstone connect important prophetic parallels to our generation? A prophecy by Christ may hold the clue to the parallels of Noah's time.

Roaring of the Sea

Jesus said that one of the signs prior to His return would come from the sea. A large percentage of the surface of the earth is water, and there are numerous seas and oceans separating the continents. Jesus warned that there would be dangerous activity occurring in the sea prior to His return.

> And there will be signs in the sun, in the moon, and in the stars; and on the earth distress of nations, with perplexity, the sea and the waves roaring (Luke 21:25).

Other translations of this verse say:

> Distress of nations, in perplexity for the roaring of the sea and the billows (*NAS*).
>
> Dismay among nations, in perplexity at the roaring of the sea and the waves (*NASB*).
>
> Distress (trouble and anguish) of nations in bewilderment and perplexity [without resources, left wanting, embarrassed, in doubt, not knowing which way to turn] at the roaring (the echo) of the tossing of the sea (*AMP*).
>
> And down here on earth the nations will be in turmoil, perplexed by the roaring seas and strange tides (*NLT*).

Men are always concerned with being in control of their lives and destiny. Numerous things in life men cannot control, however; and most involve the weather and nature.

- Men cannot control the heat the sun produces.
- Men cannot control the snow that falls.
- Men cannot control the amount of rain that falls.
- Men cannot control the waves of the sea.
- Men cannot control a hurricane that is coming from off the water.

Man may predict the path of a tornado or hurricane, project the time for a storm, or forecast when a snow squall will hit a region, but man cannot restrain the power of the weather. These powers are in the control of God and His sovereign will.

Those living on the east coast of the United States know too well man's inability to control the path of a storm, especially hurricanes!

HURRICANES ON THE SEA

Hurricanes which eventually strike the east coast of the United States usually form in the southern Atlantic Ocean, off the western coast of Africa; or in the Gulf of Mexico. They gather heat and energy through contact with warm ocean waters. The evaporation of sea water increases their power. Winds must reach a minimum of 74 miles per hour before being classified a hurricane. The storm may be 400 miles wide, and the eye is generally 20 to 30 miles wide. Hurricanes can spin for up to two weeks over open waters.

Two natural elements of nature cause a *roaring* of the sea: a tsunami and a hurricane! Moments before a tsunami strikes land, eyewitnesses describe hearing a roaring sound coming from the sea! When a hurricane moves inland, the high impact winds create a suction in and around buildings that sounds like a dull, loud roar from the wind and the water.

HURRICANES OVER FLORIDA

In 2004, the residents of Florida were stunned by four major hurricanes entering the coastlines of the state. The last time three major hurricanes spun through Florida, causing such severe weather, was in 1964, 40 years ago. The four major hurricanes were Charlie (August 14), Frances (September 5), Ivan (September 16), and Jeanne (September 25). Estimated damage in Florida was $21 billion!

The 9.0 earthquake and tsunami in December 2004 were the worst in 40 years, and the Florida hurricanes were the worst in 40 years. The last time such deadly devastation occurred was in 1964, a few months after prayer and Bible reading were removed from the public schools in North America! It is ironic that 40 years after the Supreme Court decided God was not welcome in our schools, another series of hurricanes pounded the Sunshine State. Forty in the Bible indicates a time of testing:

- It rained in Noah's day for 40 days and nights (Genesis 7:4).
- Moses was 40 days on the mount when Israel sinned (Deuteronomy 9:9-14).
- The spies came back with an evil report after 40 days (Numbers 13).
- Israel wandered through the wilderness for 40 years (Psalm 95:8-11).
- Goliath taunted Israel for 40 days (1 Samuel 17:16).
- Nineveh was given 40 days to repent (Jonah 3:4).
- Jesus fasted and was tempted by Satan for 40 days (Matthew 4:1, 2)

For these four hurricanes and a major tsunami to strike after 40 years indicates a prophetic significance to the season in which these events occurred. Our responsibility is to correctly discern the season and interpret it according to the spiritual times and seasons of America and the world.

HITTING THE COASTAL "WALLS"

In America's major coastal cities, especially where tourists converge, large surge walls are built on the beaches to protect the inland from water damage caused by storms. During the 2004 hurricanes, even the surge walls failed to protect the inland from severe water and wind damage.

The coastal areas surrounding America on both the east and west coast are considered the "walls" of our nation. In the time of the Bible the walls of the cities were fortified and served as a buffer to protect the inhabitants from invading armies and wild beasts. Enemies attacking any city knew that the city was vulnerable once the walls or gates of the city were destroyed.

In the time of Joshua, the city of Jericho was supernaturally captured when the walls surrounding the city collapsed. Over 31 Canaanite cities remained to be conquered, but only Jericho was taken. I suggest the reason the walls collapsed could be due to something placed in the walls.

Years ago, archeologists excavating the ancient ruins of Jericho discovered a jar had been placed in the mud bricks of the city wall. The contents contained the fragile dry bones of an infant. A tour guide speculated that the inhabitants of the city may have placed the bones of infants in the walls to protect the walls from enemies or spirits.

God judged the walls of Jericho! Even the actual bricks have small pieces of bones in them. These may be animal bones and not human. I believe God judged the walls of Jericho because the people had sacrificed innocent blood to protect their city.

Jerusalem's outer walls were built of stone. Because the city was built on a series of high hills, some felt it would be impossible for the holy city to be captured (Lamentations 4:12). However, both the Babylonians and the Romans struck Jerusalem with such force that they were able to topple portions of the walls and burn the city's gates. God warned Israel that invasions were coming, and told them one of the reasons the enemy would be permitted to enter the city was because the Hebrew nation had shed innocent blood!

Shedding innocent blood involved killing the prophets (Matthew 23:31), and offering their children up to idols such as Molech (Jeremiah 32:35, 36). Jesus wept over Jerusalem as He warned that His generation would receive punishment because their ancestors had shed the blood of righteous men (Matthew 23:30-35).

This was the reason Jesus gave for the coming invasion and destruction of Jerusalem. It is clear that shedding innocent blood brings a curse on the land.

> Therefore, indeed, I send you prophets, wise men, and scribes: some of them you will kill and crucify, and some of them you will scourge in your synagogues and persecute from city to city ,that on you may come all the righteous blood shed on the earth, from the blood of righteous Abel to the blood of Zechariah, son of Berechiah, whom you murdered between the temple and the altar. Assuredly, I say to you, all these things will come upon this generation (Mathew 23:34-36).

This prophecy was given about 40 years before the destruction of Jerusalem. The words indicate the reasons for the destruction of Jerusalem. Christ said His generation would experience the wrath of God for the slaying of the prophets and righteous wise men sent to warn them of their iniquities.

The walls of Jerusalem were beaten down by Roman battering rams and breaches opened the door to the enemy!

THE BEACHES WERE DEVASTATED

During the four hurricanes, many of the Florida beaches were devastated. I was in Destin weeks after the last hurricane and was shocked to see where entire sections of the beach, including the beautiful sand dunes, were completely gone, as though picked up by a giant hand and scattered miles away. Bars, hotels and beach-front properties were destroyed, and homes and apartments were ripped apart as though they were built out of toothpicks.

For some reason I immediately thought of how so many of the beaches that were destroyed were hot spots for spring breakers. Spring break attracts thousands of college students to the Florida coast for all-night parties. The days and nights are filled with heavy alcohol consumption, the use of illegal drugs, sexual promiscuity and about every sensual pleasure known to man. Hurricanes literally tore apart these hot spots on the coastal areas of the Sunshine State. We must again point out that it "rains on the just and the unjust," and many homes of good people were also affected during this season.

THE WARFARE IN THE ATMOSPHERE

> Whose voice then shook the earth: but now He has promised, saying, "Yet once more I shake not only the earth, but also heaven" (Hebrews 12:26).

There may be another reason the atmosphere has changed, creating violent shakings. What are the spiritual implications of the many storms brewing over the seas of the world? Spiritual unrest in heavenly places could also be manifesting itself on earth in the form of terrible winds and the tossing of the sea. Paul the apostle indicates that Satan is the "prince of the power of the air" (Ephesians 2:2).

Notice he didn't just say, "Prince of the air," but he said, "Prince of the *power* of the air." This Greek word *exousia* means authority or jurisdiction. The Greeks used two words for air. In Ephesians 2:2, the word alludes to the atmosphere between the ground and the clouds. This region of heaven is a stronghold for four levels of demonic spirits. They are given in Ephesians:

- Principalities
- Powers
- Rulers of the darkness of this world
- Wicked spirits in heavenly places

An example of these spirits operating in the heavenly realm is Daniel 10, where a demonic "prince of Persia" resisted an angel of the Lord from taking God's answer to prayer to the prophet Daniel (Daniel 10:1-13).

In Revelation we read that Satan and a host of spirits are now positioned in the heavenlies and will be cast down to the earth during the time of the Great Tribulation (Revelation 12:9). This conflict will create a mighty shaking in the heavenlies. It may even be the event that causes the powers of heaven to he shaken and the star of heaven to fall to the earth.

THE POWERS OF THE HEAVENS SHALL BE SHAKEN

One event to precede the return of Christ is a strange prediction concerning the powers of heaven being shaken.

> But in those days, after that tribulation, the sun shall be darkened, and the moon shall not give her light, and the stars of heaven shall fall, and the powers that are in heaven shall be shaken (Mark 13:24, 25).

In the Bible there are several meanings to the English word *powers*. There are *powers of heaven*, which alludes to the sun, moon and stars. Another word for powers identifies *a person who is a magistrate or civic ruler*. There is also a word which alludes to *spiritual powers under the dominion of Satan*.

1. When Paul said we wrestle against principalities and powers, not against flesh and blood, he referred to demonic hosts under Satan's dominion (Ephesians 6:12).

2. When Paul spoke of strong civic leaders, he often called them powers (Titus 3:1).

3. When the prophetic Scriptures speak of the powers of heaven being shaken prior to the return of Christ, this alludes to the celestial powers of the sun, moon and stars (Mark 13:25).Christ himself warned that the stars would fall from heaven and the powers of heaven would be shaken (Matthew 24:29).

While there are three definitions of the word *powers* in the Greek New Testament, there are also two meanings of the word *stars* found in the Bible. The word *stars* can be literal stars, and is also a word used to identify angels.

STARS FIGHTING IN THE HEAVENS

Judges 5 presents an example of the word *stars* alluding to angels and not the literal stars of heaven. Israel's enemy, Sisera, had gathered 900 chariots of iron and his entire army near the brook Kishon to fight against Israel. Suddenly and without warning, the brook began to flood and the chariots were swept away. The Bible says:

> They fought from the heavens; the stars from their courses fought against Sisera. The torrent of Kishon swept them away, that ancient torrent, the torrent of Kishon (Judges 5:20, 21).

Josephus, the Jewish historian, relates that just as the battle began, a violent tempest came with great torrents of rain. A devastating hailstorm drove full in the faces of the Canaanites, blinding and numbing them with cold so that they could neither use their bows with effect nor even hold their swords (Josephus, *Antiquities of the Jews*).

Scripture indicates the *stars fought in their courses.* Most commentators agree that angels of God assisted in this battle. This is the primary meaning of *stars* (angels) fighting in this passage. Other Old Testament references in the English translation of the Bible use the word *stars* as a symbol for angels (Job 38:7, Daniel 8:12). This story of Sisera indicates that a war in heaven, fought by the angels, produced a major storm on earth—literally, a flood—which swept away over 900 chariots!

The Book of Revelation indicates that in the future a similar angelic war in heaven will occur between the archangel Michael and his angels, and Satan and his angels. This violent war in the heavens concludes with Satan being cast to the earth. After Satan is expelled from his domain in the second heaven and hurled to earth, a warning is announced by an angel of the Lord:

> Therefore rejoice, O heavens, and you who dwell in them! Woe to the inhabitants of the earth and the sea! For the devil has come down to you, having great wrath, because he knows that he has a short time (Revelation 12:12).

After Satan is cast down to the earth, he produces a flood of water on earth in an attempt to destroy a large Jewish remnant being protected in the wilderness of Moab (Revelation 12:13-17). Many scholars believe this remnant is the Jews who will flee to Petra, a natural fortification in the country of Jordan. Satan will bring water like a flood to drown this chosen remnant.

I have been to Petra, and there is one entrance into the city. It is a passageway 8- to 20-feet-wide with high cliffs on both sides. This entrance is called the *siq*, and it twists and turns for over a mile. There have been times when flash floods struck the area, and on one occasion 18 French tourists were swept away. They were unable to flee the sudden surge of water pouring through the siq.

Likewise, Satan will create a supernatural flood of water to flood through the region, but somehow there will be an opening in the earth into which the water will pour (Revelation 12:16).

The future war in heaven will produce floods on earth. Even the prophet Daniel, the visionary who foresaw the time of the end, indicates that the "end shall be with a flood" (Daniel 9:26). In this passage, the word flood is *sheteph* and means a "deluge." It can allude to a literal flood of water, or to an overwhelming surge of trouble.

These passages make it clear that spiritual conflicts occurring in heavenly places have an impact on earth. The impact on earth *can* be in the form of floods. Remember the warning given to the earth after Satan is expelled from the heavens? "Woe to the inhabitants of the earth and the sea" (Revelation 12:12). Satan's discharge from his heavenly position impacts the sea!

HEAVENLY BATTLES CREATE NATURAL STORMS

It does appear that the conflict between the angels of God and the demonic powers of Satan can create strange weather patterns in the heavens that impact the inhabitants on earth. From a strictly human point of view, this would seem ludicrous. Consider the mystery of why hurricanes, hail and floods occur, however. We know the circumstances that create them, but what triggers the circumstances? It is like trying to explain creation without knowing the missing link, God, who set the events in motion.

The days of Noah produced the worst loss of life by water than at any other time in history. If the time before Christ's return is parallel to the days of Noah, we will see a huge destruction of life by water. Recently, the tsunami in the Asian rim was the largest loss of life by water since the flood of Noah!

THE FIRE OF SODOM AND GOMORRAH

In the days of Lot, five cities nestled at the southern end of the Dead Sea. They were called the cities of the plain (Genesis 19:29). These five are identified in Genesis 14:1, 2:

- Sodom
- Gomorrah
- Admah
- Zeboiim
- Zoar

Four of these five cities were suddenly destroyed by what the Bible calls "brimstone from God out of heaven" (Genesis 19:24). The Hebrew word *brimstone* alludes to a form of combustible sulfur. Geologists know that these five cities were located at the southern end of the Dead Sea in Israel, and that there is sulfur in the area. They are also aware that early historians reported eyewitnesses living in the area who wrote of seeing small fires creeping through cracks in the earth's surface and a purplish smoke occasionally forming a repulsive, sulfur-like odor near the Dead Sea.

Several miles from the suspected location of the five cities, there is a large area in Jordan, covered with volcanic rock. The signs suggest that a major volcanic eruption once occurred in the area.

The combination of subterranean fire, the sulfur content and the volcanic rock seems to indicate there was a massive volcanic eruption which once wreaked havoc on the region. As fireballs of red-hot lava shot high into the atmosphere, it would appear to an observer from a distance that fire and brimstone was falling from heaven on the cities. As Lot was leaving the city, his wife turned back to watch this phenomenon, and "became a pillar of salt" (Genesis 19:26).

For centuries, skeptics have read this passage and explained the impossibility of taking this literally. Having been to Israel over 26 times, however, I can attest to the fact that there is a huge "salt mountain" on the southwestern side of the Dead Sea. From a distance it appears to be a normal mountain, but on closer examination it is actually a large mountain of salt! The southern half of the Dead Sea is also littered with large piles of salt crystals, often two to three feet high and a foot in diameter.

Four of the five cities were consumed in fire and smoke. Today, the ruins lie encased in layers of salt under the murky, salty waters of the Dead Sea. The destruction of these cities served as a warning to future generations who would engage in similar sins. They led to the fiery destruction of the cities of the plain. Sodom and Gomorrah, and the cities around them, gave themselves over to sexual immorality and went after strange flesh. They are set forth as an example of suffering the vengeance of eternal fire (Jude 7).

The central feature of Lot's day was the destruction of these cities by fire. More than likely it was a volcanic eruption that blasted brimstone into the air, crashing down on thousands of inhabitants. Biblical prophecy does indicate future events that are in line with volcanic eruptions on earth.

And I will show wonders in the heavens and in the earth: blood and fire and pillars of smoke. The sun shall be turned into darkness, and the moon into blood, before the coming of the great and awesome day of the Lord (Joel 2:30, 31).

4

Blood, Fire and Pillars of Smoke

One of the most unusual prophecies of the future is found in the prophetic Book of Joel and the New Testament Book of Acts. In Acts 2:19, 20, the apostle Peter quotes Joel 2 concerning the last days:

> And I will show wonders in the heavens and in the earth: blood and fire and pillars of smoke. The sun shall be turned into darkness, and the moon into blood, before the coming of the great and awesome day of the Lord.

1. There will be wonders in the heavens and in the earth.
2. There will be blood.
3. There will be fire.
4. There will be pillars of smoke.

According to Luke, these important elements of prophecy are signs that will come from "the earth beneath" (Acts 2:19). A volcanic eruption is the only *natural activity* that could fulfill the allusion to blood, fire and pillars of smoke.

In the Bible, *blood* and *sword* are associated with war, or extreme suffering. The word *fire* is self-explanatory, since every volcanic eruption originates from the molten, fiery core of the earth. An eruption is accompanied by huge, dark clouds ascending into heaven, forming the shape of a pillar, or a *pillar of smoke*.

In the Old Testament, the Hebrew word for *pillars* is often used in connection with the pillars of the Tabernacle, the Temple of Solomon or the structure of a building (Exodus 38; 1 Kings 7). When the word *pillars* alludes to a building, the Hebrew common word is *ammuwd*, which means a "standing column." Only two places in the Old Testament mention pillars of smoke (Song of Solomon 3:6 and Joel 2:30). In both references the Hebrew word for pillars is *tiymarah*, which means a *column or a cloud*.

Throughout history, entire cities and communities have been wiped out by a major volcanic eruption. Hundreds of thousands of small and large dormant volcanoes are scattered throughout the world, and especially in the Pacific Rim. Even in the United States, Mount St. Helens in Washington State erupted as recently as 1980, and began stirring again in 2004. Any major earthquake or shifting of the plates could stir fresh movement among lifeless volcanoes throughout the world.

Prior to and during the 7-year Tribulation, volcanic activity will definitely re-surface in selective areas of the world. A strange prophecy in the Book of Revelation could allude to a huge volcanic eruption:

> The second angel sounded: and something like a great mountain burning with fire was thrown into the sea, and a third of the sea became blood. And a third of the living creatures in the sea died, and a third of the ships were destroyed (Revelation 8:8, 9).

This mountain burning with fire could be located in a coastal area, on a large island in one of the world's major seas, or it may be an undersea volcano. As the mountain explodes into a deadly volcanic eruption, the lava, smoke and volcanic ash will begin to fill the sea and disrupt the ecosystem. The impact of the eruption will create huge waves (tsunamis) which will literally overturn a third of the ships in the sea. The majority of the world's ships are fishing vessels and not battleships.

During a major tsunami, fish are pulled into the mighty currents and are thrown up on the shores of the islands. Any major volcanic eruption causes the waters nearby to become highly acidic and undrinkable. Pam and I once watched a video at home that dealt with a volcanic eruption in the northwestern United States. We had assumed that the danger was in the molten lava burning trees or houses. We were amazed to learn that the volcanic ash and smoke are deadly, and the waters became undrinkable.

VOLCANOES IN AMERICA AND EUROPE

It may come as a shock to those in the United States, but America has 68 potentially active volcanoes, more than any other other country except Indonesia and Japan. Every year at least six of them begin to belch smoke. Because some are located in Hawaii and Alaska, few people take notice.

One major volcano outside of America is located in the Mediterranean Sea, between Sicily and Italy. The volcano, Mount Vesuvius, is part of a super volcano named "Somma." Mount Vesuvius is the same volcano that erupted in 79 A.D., burying the cities of Pompeii and Herculaneum. The mountain continued to erupt every 100 years until about 1037 A.D., when it entered a 600-year period of quiescence. In 1631, the volcano erupted again, killing an additional 4,000 unsuspecting inhabitants.

Pliny the Younger observed the eruption of 79 A.D. from approximately seven miles away (21 km). He wrote a graphic description of the explosive eruption:

> For several days before (the eruption) the earth had been shaken, but this fact did not cause fear because this was a feature commonly observed in Campania . . . [The plume] resembled a [Mediterranean] pine more than any other tree. Like a very high tree, the cloud went high and expanded in different branches. It expanded laterally, sometimes white, sometimes dark and stained by the sustained sand and ash.
>
> Further on, we saw the sea retreating as if pushed by the earthquakes.

A similar tsunami was described at the beginning of the eruption of Vesuvius in 1631. This volcano could fulfill a prophecy in Revelation 17. John tells of a city which, in his day, was reigning over the kings of the earth (Revelation 17:18). This city, called Mystery Babylon (Revelation 17:5), has been identified by scholars for centuries as the city of Rome, Italy. Toward the end of the 7-year Tribulation, this city will be destroyed in an hour (Revelation 18:10).

The city of prophecy will be burned with fire, and merchantmen and their ships will remain at a distance for fear of the smoke (Revelation 18:15-18). This one-hour destruction could come from a major nuclear warhead or from a massive volcanic eruption which wipes out the entire city in 60 minutes. In either instance, the smoke of the destruction would keep men at a distance for fear of radiation or the volcanic ash.

Another area of great concern is the volcanoes lying around the Pacific Rim. This rim has been called the "Ring of Fire" by vulcanologists. The Asian continent and islands are in great danger of future volcanic activity, especially if there is a change in the shifting of the earth's plates, and other major earthquakes around volcanic areas.

THE VOLCANO AND WORMWOOD

After John revealed how a burning mountain will impact marine life, he then heard from the angel of the Lord that a meteorite will strike the earth and pollute the waters, causing a third of the drinking waters to become undrinkable. This falling star is named *wormwood,* because the waters become too bitter to drink (Revelation 8:11).

As pointed out earlier, with such future dangers surrounding the coastal areas and the seas, is it any wonder that men will flee from the big cities and the coastal areas and run to the mountains (Revelation 6:15-16)?

A volcanic eruption could also easily fulfill the prophecy recorded 2,500 years ago by the prophet Joel, concerning the fire and pillars of smoke. Volcanic eruptions are a parallel of the days of Lot and the destruction of the four wicked cities.

The Water and the Fire

In Noah's day the earth was covered with water and in Lot's time four of five cities were burned with fire. In Noah's day only he, his wife, their three sons and their wives (8 people) escaped the universal flood.

In Lot's day, only he and his two daughters escaped the destruction of the cities. The only city among the five that was spared was a small city called Zoar. God spared Zoar because Lot intended to flee to Zoar for refuge from the burning cities of the plain (Genesis 19:20-23).

Noah survived the judgment by water and Lot escaped the judgment by fire. The tsunami of 2004 sent over 200,000 people to their deaths by waves of water. It was the largest number of deaths by water since the days of Noah! Was this an early sign that we are truly entering the days similar to the days of Noah?

America was attacked on 9-11 with planes being used as bombs. The Twin Towers and the Pentagon burned with fire and thousands of lives were lost in the deadliest terrorist attack in American history.

More Warnings of Things To Come

Russian scientists recently warned that the entire planet has entered a period of seismic activity. Weaknesses in the earth's crust cause it to break apart, creating eruptions, major earthquakes and geysers. *Pravda*, the Russian newspaper, quoted a Professor Dolginov who warned that countries surrounding the equator will be susceptible to major quakes in the near future. He believes that future tsunamis will be "three to five times more severe than [the 2004] one:"

> According to our theory, there exists latitudinal lineaments (cracks of the earth's core), which pose potential danger in terms of seismic activity. If we are to follow the equatorial crack westward of South East Asia, we could expect rather serious seismic cataclysms in Equatorial Guinea, Cameroon, Nigeria, and Gabon.

The theory, called the Angular Momentum Theory, says the earth has become more wobbly, and there is a strong possibility of a polar inversion. For example, the North Pole could become the South Pole and vice versa. The scientist also noted that the ancient Mayan civilization warned that around 2012 the entire world would face major natural calamities from natural disasters.

Prophetic Scriptures, as we have indicated, already give an amazing preview of future destruction and disasters to the planet that matches many of the human predictions by geologists, seismologists and scientists. A massive volcanic eruption would fulfill the picture of the blood, fire and pillars of smoke seen by the prophet Joel. How strange that earthquakes, tsunamis and volcanic eruptions are the visible manifestations of a planet in travail and agony, awaiting the day its Creator returns to deliver creation from the curse of sin and death.

In late 2003, a swarm of small earthquakes struck 19 miles (30 kilometers) below Lake Tahoe, which straddles the border of California and Nevada. At the same time, Slide Mountain, 11 miles (18 kilometers) away in Nevada, moved dramatically, according to satellite readings. Scientists were puzzled. They suspected that the two events were related, but the earthquakes were too small and too deep to cause the mountain to move. Something else was at play.

The answer was magma. Scientists were astonished to discover that an injection of magma, or molten rock, into the lower crust of the earth had caused both the earthquakes and the movement of the mountain.

"This is the first time we have seen anything like this," said Geoffrey Blewitt, a research professor at the Nevada Bureau of Mines and Geology at the University of Nevada in Reno.

This is what the Lord Almighty, the God of Israel says: "You saw the great disaster I brought on Jerusalem. . . . They provoked me to anger. . . . Again and again I sent my servants . . . but they did not listen or pay attention (Jeremiah 44:2-5).

5

Selective Judgment

Prior to the beginning of the final 7-year Tribulation, there will be what I term "selective judgments" on certain areas, leaving other regions untouched. I base this on the story of Lot. God was willing to spare Sodom and Gomorrah if He could find 10 righteous people (Genesis 18:32). The Lord found only four, and one looked back while fleeing. Of the five cities, four of them were destroyed.

Oddly, one small city, Zoar, was spared from destruction. Throughout history, even in times of judgment, God has provided places of refuge and safe havens from the trouble around His people.

- Noah was secure in the ark, and Lot was safe in Zoar.
- The Hebrews survived famine in Egypt and were later preserved in the wilderness from starvation and beasts!
- In Ezekiel's day the righteous were marked with special protection, while the unrighteous suffered at the hands of the invaders (Ezekiel 9).

According to historians, prior to the Roman armies invading Jerusalem, many Christians fled the city and crossed the mountains into Pella, Jordan. This small community became a safe haven for Christians, who later built a large church and Christian community in the region. In times of judgment, God often warns believers and gives them a plan of survival, or a plan of escape. He has always protected His people.

As we enter the time of the end, there will be *more* birth pains, as creation travails, waiting to be delivered. There will be seasons of selective judgment, where one area will experience a severe trial and other areas will seem untouched. Through it all, there is a divine purpose for these events.

The Ultimate Purpose

The history of Israel, as recorded in the Bible, reveals the reason for natural disasters and trouble—to lead men to repent. After a disaster, a national tragedy or an act of judgment occurs, the response from spiritually minded people can be summed up in three main reactions:

1. The first reaction is *reflection.*
2. The second reaction is *repentance.*
3. The third reaction is *restoration.*

A Time of Reflection

Sudden trouble always creates the opportunity for reflection, or inner searching of the human heart and soul. After the initial shock of the difficulty wears off, questions begin to rise like steam from a hot spring in wintertime. *Why did this event happen? Why couldn't God intervene? Why were innocent lives taken? What was the purpose of such a tragedy?*

When massive numbers of deaths occur in a single or a series of disasters, men and women become more aware of their own mortality. They realize that death eventually comes to all living creatures, and sooner or later their name will be on the list. This time of reflection often leads to a personal search for what is beyond this life. Reflection is often most intense after extreme trouble strikes a person's life.

Once while ministering, I asked a large congregation how many would never have come to know Christ as Savior had trouble not come to them. I was amazed when over half of the congregation raised their hands. I got the same reaction when I repeated the question in numerous other churches in North America.

The same can be said about the men and women who are incarcerated in prisons and detention centers across America. Many come to Christ after they have committed a crime. They realize they must make a change in their lives or they will repeat the same crime—or one similar.

Eventually, the seed of the gospel penetrates the hard soil of the heart and from the barren womb of spiritual death come the flowers of new life! When Israel was in captivity in Babylon, the Jews reflected on their past lives in Jerusalem:

> By the rivers of Babylon, there we sat down, yea, we wept when we remembered Zion. We hung our harps upon the willows in the midst of it. For there those who carried us away captive asked of us a song, and those who plundered us requested mirth, saying, "Sing us one of the songs of Zion!"
> How shall we sing the Lord's song in a foreign land? If I forget you, O Jerusalem, let my right hand forget its skill! If I do not remember you, let my tongue

> cling to the roof of my mouth—if I do not exalt Jerusalem above my chief joy (Psalm 137:1-6).

A period of inner reflection will result in either a hardness of the heart, as in the case of the Pharaoh of Egypt, or lead to a path of repentance and a return to God.

A Time of Repentance

To repent means to turn around. A person must repent if he or she is headed in the wrong direction. The Biblical definition of sin is "missing the mark." It implies a person who has a bow and is aiming to hit a certain spot, but the arrow veers off in the wrong direction.

In life, it is easy to be sidetracked by lust of the flesh, the lust of the eyes and the pride of life. These things cause us to miss the mark (1 John 2:16). When we repent we change our way of thinking and reconsider our ways in the light of God's ways. Repentance leads to a time of spiritual renewal and refreshing.

> Repent therefore and be converted, that your sins may be blotted out, so that times of refreshing may come from the presence of the Lord (Acts 3:19).

The Greek word in Acts 3:19 for *refreshing* means, "to obtain relief." It implies "to make cool." Do you remember when you first received Christ? Remember how the burden of sin was lifted, and you felt spiritually light and free? Many people have described their conversion as a feeling of taking a bath in cool, clean water . . . and coming up clean!

When a believer sins and repents, a season of refreshing always accompanies salvation. Old Testament prophets understood that God's blessings could come to the nation if the people repented of their evil ways. When Daniel was in Babylonian captivity, he was reading the scroll of the prophet Jeremiah. He read where the Jews would be in Babylonian captivity for 70 years (Jeremiah 25:11).

In Daniel 9, the prophet began interceding to God on behalf of his people, the Jews. He confessed their sins and the sins of their fathers. The prayer was interrupted by the angel Gabriel who revealed that Israel would return and rebuild their nation. When a people or a nation reflects, returns to God and repents of their sins, they will then experience complete restoration and blessing from God!

A Time of Restoration

God promised Israel that He would "restore the years" the enemy had taken from them (Joel 2:25).

> I will restore to you the years that the swarming locust has eaten, the crawling locust, the consuming locust and the chewing locust. My great army which I sent among you. You shall eat in plenty and be satisfied, and praise the name of the Lord your God, who has dealt wondrously with you; and My people shall never be put to shame (Joel 2:25, 26).

Twice, Jerusalem was destroyed by armies, and the Hebrews were led away, dispersed among the Gentile nations. The first time was during Nebuchadnezzar's reign in Babylon, and the second was in 70 A.D. under the Roman Tenth Legion. Both times, the Hebrews returned to their land and began to rebuild the desolate places. Recently, Israel was restored as a nation in 1948, after being nonexistent for over 1,870 years.

After every disaster comes a rebuilding and a restoration process. This is true with every nation and catastrophic event of the world, including the terrorist attacks in New York on 9/11. The question is, will the future times of trouble and tribulation lead the nations to turn to God, or will they refuse to repent of their sins as they will do in the Great Tribulation?

> They blasphemed the God of heaven because of their pains and their sores, and did not repent of their deeds (Revelation 16:11).

Those who repent will find favor with God—both in this life and in the life to come. Remember, the time of Great Tribulation is a set period of only seven years. Eternity, however, is forever. We must discern these signs of the times, and live in expectation of the return of Christ to earth. Truly, we are in the beginning of the last days of Bible prophecy!

Let us hear the conclusion of the whole matter: Fear God and keep His commandments, for this is man's all. For God will bring every work into judgment, including every secret thing, whether good or evil (Ecclesiastes 12:13, 14).

6

Conclusion

Whenever there is a global event of Biblical proportions, I often receive emails or letters asking if I believe this event was the breaking of one of the seals in the Book of Revelation, or if it was the early initiation of the 7-year Tribulation recorded in the Book of Revelation.

I remind people that throughout history there have been major wars and signs. Events such as the holocaust in which six million Jews died, were previews of coming events. Such terrible tragedies give the discerning believer a mini-preview of the major events that will follow!

The events presently transpiring are an increase in the birth pains. The world has not yet entered the time of the Great Tribulation. There will be an increase in the signs of Christ's return and an increase in both the number and intensity of the natural disasters. They will begin to strike the globe in various places.

It would be easy for a person to become quite discouraged and even slightly oppressed when he considers what the Biblical prophets have written concerning the last days and the time of the end. We should, however, remember that this time of Tribulation will last only for a period of seven years, and will climax in the visible return of Christ to rule and reign on earth for 1,000 years.

The world will then enter a time of great peace and prosperity under the leadership of Jesus Christ our Lord. Until then, it is our assignment to bring a message of reflection, repentance and restoration.

Appendix 1

The Protection of the Righteous

> Blessed is he who considers the poor; the Lord will deliver him in time of trouble. The Lord will preserve him and keep him alive, and he will be blessed on the earth; You will not deliver him to the will of his enemies (Psalm 41:1, 2).

Numerous Scriptural promises of the righteous being protected in times of trouble are found throughout the Bible. Righteous souls were either delivered from the trouble before it occurred, or were supernaturally preserved in the midst of the trouble. Noah was preserved in the Ark *during* the flood, and Lot was delivered out of the city *before* its destruction.

> The Lord shall preserve you from all evil; He shall preserve your soul. The Lord shall preserve your going out and your coming in (Psalms 121:7, 8).

Missionaries who traveled to the areas where the tsunamis struck were amazed to hear the remarkable stories from Christians. God supernaturally protected the lives of His people during the time of this disaster. Pastor Tom Oothuppan from Sri Lanka e-mailed missionary Rusty Domingue on Januray 11, 2005. He told of a village that had 100 families of born-again believers. Many of the homes were close to the sea and most lost their possessions, including household articles, equipment for their jobs and other important items. The believers were rejoicing that their lives were spared.

Missionary Luke Walters told several amazing stories from Sri Lanka. In one area of the country a pastor was continually persecuted and beaten for the gospel. One man was primarily responsible for the persecution. After the tsunami, it was discovered that the persecutor's entire family, including relatives, were killed in the disaster.

One evening the pastor heard someone wailing and travailing, weeping uncontrollably. He investigated, and discovered it was the man who had persecuted the pastor and had lost his entire family. The man repented, crying, "I lost my family because I attacked the true man of God and the true God!" The poor fellow recognized that his mistreatments of the righteous brought trouble to his own house.

In the New Testament, Herod had James killed and Peter arrested. The proud leader organized a parade in which he was called a "god" by the frenzied crowd. Suddenly an angel of the Lord struck him, and he fell over sick. In five days he was dead, and worms ate into his intestines (Acts 12:21-23). When a sorcerer named Elymas came against Paul and attempted to stop him from preaching and converting a deputy, Elymus was instantly stricken with blindness—a judgment against him for hindering the message of the gospel (Acts 13:7-12).

As the church approaches the last days, the Almighty will not permit the gospel message to be watered down or hindered from being proclaimed to the nations. Those who persecute, kill and attempt to stop the preaching of the gospel will encounter the wrath of God. The Lord not only protects His people, He also preserves them.

> You shall not be afraid of the terror by night, nor of the arrow that flies by day, nor of the pestilence that walks in darkness, nor of the destruction that lays waste at noonday. A thousand may fall at your side, and ten thousand at your right hand; but it shall not come near you (Psalm 91:5-7).

Missionary Walters also told of a church located on a hill not far from the sea. As the tsunami swept through, many Christians ran into the church, removing their shoes before entering (a custom in many Asian countries). Someone closed the door and the waters began rising. After the water receded, they discovered that everyone outside of the church was dead, but the water in the building only rose six inches. Even their shoes outside the doors were still there!

Several major newspapers reported that the director of an orphanage filled a boat up with the children from his compound and managed to ride out the tsunami. Prayer kept the boat from overturning and drowning the innocent orphans that he and his wife were caring for.

Just as Simon Peter cried out when he was sinking, "Lord save me," and was rescued from the cold waters that surrounded him, powerful testimonies tell how prayer and crying out to God helped bring a miraculous deliverance to many Christians in the nations where the tsunami struck.

Not every story will have such an amazing ending, as some Christians also lost their lives in this event. The good news for them is they have gone to be with the Lord, and their "battle is over!" For the survivors it is a time to reflect, repent and restore.

Appendix 2

Warnings from the Animals

Thousands of people could have been spared during the 2004 tsunami had the people on the beaches and on the islands watched the actions of the animals. Those who toured the ruins of the devastation were amazed to find that few animals were killed by the water. Animals reacted by moving away from the shore and to higher ground *before* the waves crashed ashore.

For centuries, people have noticed that when cattle lie on the ground, it is a sign of rain. Dogs begin barking wildly and acting frantic before an earthquake. Even snakes, according to researchers in China, have been observed slithering out of their dens and out of hibernation just prior to an earthquake.

During the past 50 years, the Chinese have been studying snakes and Africans have been studying elephants to observe their patterns prior to major storms and earthquakes. An amazing report from Sri Lanka and Thailand involved eyewitnesses to the strange behavior of elephants before the tsunami struck.

At the Yala National Park in Sri Lanka, people saw elephants running away from the shore to higher ground about an hour before the tsunami came! Some of them had tourists on their backs, but they headed to higher ground. Amazingly, this protected the tourists from the low-lying areas and the destructive, deadly waters.

Part of the explanation is that animals have a much higher sense of smell and hearing. Dogs can be trained to sniff for drugs, and can even track down a criminal through the scent on his clothes, because the scent membranes inside a dog's nose are four times larger than in a human's. A dog's nose has 200 million scent receptors, compared to five million in a human. Some believe dogs have about 10,000 times more sensitivity to smell than a human's nose. Elephants are said to have incredible hearing, as well as infra-sound. They hear at a lower frequency than humans do.

Cats have been known to get lost on a family vacation and travel hundreds of miles to find their way back to their original homes some months later. This has been a mystery for centuries, but cats have an amazing sense of direction. Some call it "built-in radar!"

According to a director at the National Park in Sri Lanka, birds, monkeys and dogs were all acting strange on the morning of December 26, just before the tsunami hit. Other stories have surfaced about bats, which normally sleep upside down during the day, were seen flying around 30 minutes before the disaster.

For centuries, liberal scholars who do not take the Bible literally, have noted the passage where Noah took the animals into the ark. God instructed His patriarch to allow seven of each kind of animal into the ark, except the unclean animals which went in two by two, both male and female (Genesis 7:2-9). For centuries the question has been, "How could Noah have gathered all of the species of animals required to live in the ark and repopulate the earth after the flood?"

After the ark was completed God informed Noah that in seven days the flood would come (Genesis 7:4). At the conclusion of seven days, the waters in the heavens poured down and the underground springs broke forth as tons of water gushed like a violent and uncontrollable geyser. By this time

Noah, his family and the animals were safe inside the floating houseboat.

I have heard many stories of animals running to higher ground, away from rising water. Could it be possible that seven days before the flood broke loose on the earth, rumblings within the earth and an atmospheric change caused the animals in the region to seek higher ground? Perhaps they sought the very ground where Noah and his sons built the ark. We are uncertain where this was, although it took a substantial amount of wood from trees to make the floating zoo.

In 373 B.C., historians recorded that animals—rats, snakes and weasels—deserted the Greek city of Helice in droves just days before a quake devastated the place. Accounts of similar animal behavior have surfaced across the centuries. It has been reported that catfish move violently, chickens stop laying eggs and bees leave their hives in a panic.

Countless pet owners claim to have witnessed their cats and dogs acting strangely before an earthquake—barking or whining for no apparent reason, or showing signs of nervousness and restlessness. If the animals sensed danger, as we know they do, perhaps they were naturally drawn to the Ark.

Noah had little if any difficulty in selecting animals necessary to fulfill God's commandment to preserve life on earth. I am certain more people will pay attention to the animals in the future, especially if they live by the seas or ocean.

Appendix 3

America's Tsunami Threats

At the time I was a child, and because it was years ago, few Americans may remember the tsunami that struck in Alaska about 40 years ago. Geologists and scientists are now looking at the possibility of a tsunami that could impact the Atlantic ocean and affect the east coast of the United States.

One area of concern is the region of the Canary Islands. If a volcano erupted in the Canary Islands, it could cause a massive landslide on the island of La Palma and trigger tsunami waves in the Atlantic ocean. According to a 1999 report of scientists from the University College of London, such an eruption could trigger waves upward to 164 feet high. Such a massive wave would cover the east coast of the United States and could reach all the way to New York City. Some are not as concerned, since their computer models for the past 200,000 years show that the land would simply drop into the ocean and create little if any impact.

Perhaps America's greatest concerns may lie on the west coast. As the death and destruction toll from the tsunami that struck much of Southeast Asia continues to mount, attention is focusing on the Pacific Ocean. Scientists say that huge tsunamis are much more likely to develop in the Pacific Ocean than in the Indian Ocean. That's because the Pacific Ocean has many more subduction zones, which produce the most powerful earthquakes and tsunamis.

Knowing the danger, Pacific Rim countries have set up a sophisticated warning system. They hope the system will keep the death toll from a potential giant tsunami far lower in the Pacific Ocean than it was in the Indian Ocean. There, over 200,000 people were killed by the recent tsunami.

If one struck, residents along North America's Pacific coast would have very little time to get to higher ground.

"If a magnitude 9 earthquake were to strike in the Pacific Northwest and generate a tsunami, we'd have less than 15 minutes warning [before it hit the shore]," said Robert Yeats, professor emeritus of geo-sciences at Oregon State University in Corvallis.